Pearls

Ja'Lexis Posey

Copyright © 2020 by Ja'Lexis Posey
All rights reserved. No part of this book may be reproduced, scanned, or distributed in any printed or electronic form without permission.
First Edition: September 2020
Printed in the United States of America

Acknowledgments

To my grandma, Mary Jones. God knows I wish you were here to see me release this project, but I know you are here with me spiritually. I just want to thank you for everything you have done for me, and for teaching me right from wrong.

To my handsome grandfather, Elijah Posey. You just don't understand how much I miss you. I'm crying right now as I write this. I just want to thank you for always pushing me to do my best. The conversations we used to have were so life changing. You taught me how to keep a job, to never stop grinding and to always hustle. I remember the very last conversation we had like it was yesterday. You said to me, "Judy, as you go on to your next chapter, remain focused and never give up on your dreams."

And lastly, to my beautiful aunt, Virginia Robinson. I know you would be very proud of me. I listened to you and got in touch with Gin Gin. She has been a really big help! I want to thank you for always believing in me, and for telling me to keep going and to never give up!
I love you all, my beautiful angels. You are truly missed.

Introduction

Pearl: a beautiful, hard, glistening object that empowers women to create their own style statements.

Empowerment (noun): the process of becoming strong. To make confident; especially in controlling one's life and claiming one's rights.

The word *"Pearls"* very much stands out. My quote "No matter what anyone says or thinks, you are a **PEARL**", means that you are a woman who is not afraid to take any risks. You are one of a kind, and you are a woman who can turn her wounds into wisdom. Take your pain and turn it into strength.

FAITH IN GOD WILL ELEVATE YOU TO NEXT LEVEL BLESSINGS.

Many women in this world today are just afraid. They **FEAR** a lot of things. Fear can be a long-time companion, as well as an obstacle between you and your next chapter. Let your life reflect the faith you have in God. Fear nothing and pray about everything.

You are strong! Everyone goes through difficulties in life, but it's important to still stand strong, and know your self-worth.

KNOW YOUR
self-worth.

Pearls give a woman wisdom. They help you get stronger and wiser for every life experience you go through. Pearls are a valuable treasure that need no polishing. Pearls can also be used to defend against negative energy. Negative energy can be a person or situation. Regardless of what it is, it important that you don't let it bring you down. Elevate yourself like Maya Angelou says in her poem '*'Still I Rise'*'. Rise and keep going, and don't ever look back.

Stay away from those who cannot own up to their actions and those who make you feel terrible for being angry at them when you have done nothing wrong. Unhappy, bitter people drag you down to their level. Just ignore them. Don't say anything. Don't invite any parts of them into your space. Some people are awesome manipulators who cheat, lie, treat you horribly and manage to make it seem like it's all your fault. They can't function without negativity, and bringing others down makes them feel amazing.

Ask Yourself, "Do I Deserve This?"

> *"Never let someone with the significance of a speed bump become a roadblock."*

Ladies if you're in a bad situation, ONLY YOU CAN GET YOURSELF OUT! Put your foot down! In life today, both women and teen girls go through a lot. Some deal with issues like depression, issues that negatively impact their self-esteem, long-term bullying, and being the witness or victim of violence, including physical or sexual abuse. There's only so much a person can take, and with so much happening, it can definitely begin to take a toll on one mentally. If you or someone you know finds yourself in this predicament, be empowered. Try taking a walk, reading books, or meditating to redirect your thoughts.

It's All About Trust…

Toxic relationships are not healthy. No one on this earth is perfect. You have to be able to work with one another. Require more of yourself and more from your partner.

No matter what **ANYONE SAYS** *or* **THINKS,** *You are a Pearl."*
— Ja'Lexis Posey

You have to forgive some people. Most likely if they hurt you, they don't care if you forgive them or if you are still mad about the situation. The way you take your power back is through FORGIVENESS. You can't let those who quit on you, make you want to quit on yourself. I know it hurts when the ones you count on, count you out; or when the same ones you helped, won't lend you a helping hand. You have to understand it's not right, but it is life. Just because you did right by helping them, doesn't mean they will return the favor. True colors always get revealed when it's real.

Stop letting people control your life. Remember if it's not adding to your life, then you don't have to keep it in your life. Don't leave yourself open to a person who puts you last; and don't give people positions in your life that they don't deserve.

STOP BEING *the* **GO-TO PERSON FOR A PERSON YOU** *can never go to!*

Some people do not come into your life to love you, they come to use you.

Self-love is the best love. Self-love means having a high regard for your own well-being and happiness. Invest in yourself.

Most women are disgusted with the way they look and fight with insecurities, not realizing how beautiful they really are. Loving yourself is a win-win for everyone. Develop self-esteem and inner strength by building confidence. Doing this will help you to make better choices and healthier decisions in all areas of your life.

It's important to take care of business, and not sacrifice yourself in place of others.

Fully accept your TRUE SELF. Embrace the beautiful being that you are. Release any grudges that you have about loving yourself. You must accept you for you!

No matter what you do, you should always love yourself with the same strength. Everyone wants to be loved on and some think that means we need others. No!

Seek love from yourself.

ARE YOU BEING YOU FOR YOU *or* **WHO THE WORLD** *wants you to be?*

Empowerment

Empowerment is what takes place when you are becoming stronger and more confident. In our society today, we need a voice for women and young girls, someone who can teach them how to boost their self-esteem and love themselves.

Empowerment of women is for the all around development of society and the nation as a whole. We as women can both empower and learn from one another. Empowering girls and women shouldn't be an option, you should just do it. We should help each other to be the best that we can be. We should motivate each other! We are all a team, so we should stick with one another. One of the ways we can do this is by providing good information and education to girls. In doing this, they will be able to take care of themselves without needing anyone else. Your act of reaching out to someone, could be the saving grace in their life.

A young woman should be independent, responsible, and strong. There are youth services that can help them learn how to tackle life's challenges and live a more productive life. If you're not able to help them, refer them to these services.

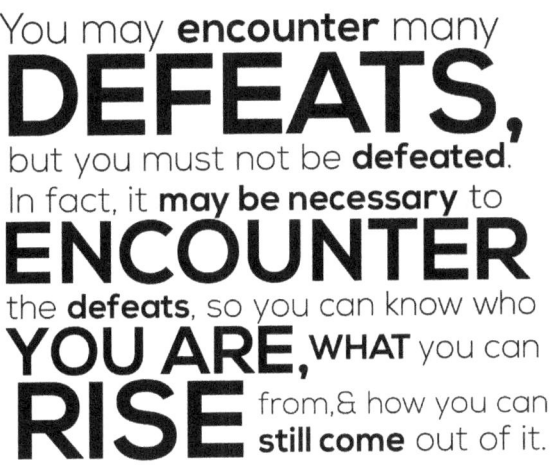

You may **encounter** many **DEFEATS,** but you must not be **defeated.** In fact, it **may be necessary** to **ENCOUNTER** the **defeats**, so you can know who **YOU ARE, WHAT** you can **RISE** from,& how you can **still come** out of it.

— Maya Angelou

5 Goals of Empowerment

1.) Positive Sense of Self
2.) Self-control
3.) Decision Making Skills
4.) Moral System of Belief
5.) Connecting

Positive Sense of Self: when you have confidence in yourself, you are able to take leadership and have compassion for others

Self-control: the ability to control your emotions, thoughts and behavior

Decision Making: guides your ability to make the right decisions

Moral System of Beliefs: gauges the standards you set for yourself; how you handle things; being responsible

Connecting: having a connection with others

12 Ways to Empower Yourself

1. Have faith in GOD.
2. Remember that "anything is possible if you believe."
3. **Take leadership.** If there's something you don't like, start with yourself and make changes.
4. Be brave.
5. **Never stop gaining amazing information.** Be a life learner who always wants to change the world and find happiness.
6. Say "no" to things that don't serve us.
7. Tell yourself you got this!
8. Learn from your pain. No matter what you've struggled through in the past, empower yourself by learning from the experience.
9. Stay around positive people ONLY!
10. Accept that you are beautiful no matter what!
11. Ground yourself.
12. Always say, "You can do it, and you can get through it." Never say you can't.

Stop waiting for the **LIGHT** at the end of the **TUNNEL** and *light it yourself.*

Women's Empowerment- the process in which women recreate what it is that they can be, do and accomplish in a circumstance that they were previously denied

Define the following words in your own way:

Confidence
_____
_____
_____
_____

Success
_____
_____
_____
_____

Power
_____
_____
_____

Faith

_____
_____
_____

Compassionate

_____
_____
_____

Unstoppable

_____
_____
_____

Love

_____
_____
_____
_____

Strength

_____
_____
_____
_____

Trust

_____
_____
_____
_____

Purpose

Questions

Do you have faith in yourself? Yes or no. If no, why?

_____

_____

_____

_____

_____

_____

Can you do it? Yes or no. If no, why?

_____

_____

_____

_____

_____

_____

Do you love yourself? Yes or no. If no, why?

_____

_____

_____

_____

_____

What do you see when you look in the mirror?

_____

_____

_____

_____

_____

What situation(s) have you gone through that led to depression? Depression meaning a persistent feeling of sadness.

_____
_____
_____
_____
_____
_____

What can you change to make you feel like you again?

_____
_____
_____
_____
_____
_____

Do you have faith in GOD?
_____
_____
_____
_____
_____
_____

For the next 30 days, write about how you are feeling. Be honest with yourself, no one can see this but you.

How are you feeling?

_____
_____
_____
_____

What are you feeling?

_____
_____
_____
_____

What negative or positive thoughts are going through your head?

_____
_____
_____
_____

What areas do you need a push in?

_____

_____

_____

_____

What are your strengths and/or weaknesses?

_____

_____

_____

_____

Do you rely on what others think of you? Yes or no? If yes, why?

_____

_____

_____

_____

Are you looking for validation (approval) from others?

_____

_____

_____

_____

Have you ever thought about harming yourself? If so, why?

_____

_____

_____

_____

How are you feeling?

_____
_____
_____
_____

What are you feeling?

_____
_____
_____
_____

What negative or positive thoughts are going through your head?

_____
_____
_____
_____

What areas do you need a push in?

_____

_____

_____

_____

What are your strengths and/or weaknesses?

_____

_____

_____

_____

Do you rely on what others think of you? Yes or no? If yes, why?

_____

_____

_____

_____

Are you looking for validation (approval) from others?

_____

_____

_____

_____

Have you ever thought about harming yourself? If so, why?

_____

_____

_____

_____

How are you feeling?

_____

_____

_____

_____

What are you feeling?

_____

_____

_____

_____

What negative or positive thoughts are going through your head?

_____

_____

_____

_____

What areas do you need a push in?

_____

_____

_____

_____

What are your strengths and/or weaknesses?

_____

_____

_____

_____

Do you rely on what others think of you? Yes or no? If yes, why?

_____

_____

_____

_____

Are you looking for validation (approval) from others?

_____

_____

_____

_____

Have you ever thought about harming yourself? If so, why?

_____

_____

_____

_____

How are you feeling?

_____
_____
_____
_____

What are you feeling?

_____
_____
_____
_____

What negative or positive thoughts are going through your head?

_____
_____
_____
_____

What areas do you need a push in?

_____

_____

_____

_____

What are your strengths and/or weaknesses?

_____

_____

_____

_____

Do you rely on what others think of you? Yes or no? If yes, why?

_____

_____

_____

_____

Are you looking for validation (approval) from others?

_____

_____

_____

_____

Have you ever thought about harming yourself? If so, why?

_____

_____

_____

Day 5

How are you feeling?

_____

_____

_____

_____

What are you feeling?

_____

_____

_____

_____

What negative or positive thoughts are going through your head?

_____

_____

_____

_____

What areas do you need a push in?

_____

_____

_____

_____

What are your strengths and/or weaknesses?

_____

_____

_____

_____

Do you rely on what others think of you? Yes or no? If yes, why?

_____

_____

_____

_____

Are you looking for validation (approval) from others?

_____

_____

_____

_____

Have you ever thought about harming yourself? If so, why?

_____

_____

_____

_____

How are you feeling?
_____
_____
_____
_____

What are you feeling?
_____
_____
_____
_____

What negative or positive thoughts are going through your head?
_____
_____
_____
_____

What areas do you need a push in?

_____

_____

_____

_____

What are your strengths and/or weaknesses?

_____

_____

_____

_____

Do you rely on what others think of you? Yes or no? If yes, why?

_____

_____

_____

_____

Are you looking for validation (approval) from others?

_____

_____

_____

_____

Have you ever thought about harming yourself? If so, why?

_____

_____

_____

_____

How are you feeling?

_____

_____

_____

_____

What are you feeling?

_____

_____

_____

_____

What negative or positive thoughts are going through your head?

_____

_____

_____

_____

What areas do you need a push in?

_____

_____

_____

_____

What are your strengths and/or weaknesses?

_____

_____

_____

_____

Do you rely on what others think of you? Yes or no? If yes, why?

_____

_____

_____

_____

Are you looking for validation (approval) from others?
_____
_____
_____
_____

Have you ever thought about harming yourself? If so, why?
_____
_____
_____
_____

Day 8

How are you feeling?

_____
_____
_____

What are you feeling?

_____
_____
_____

What negative or positive thoughts are going through your head?

_____
_____
_____

What areas do you need a push in?

_____

_____

_____

What are your strengths and/or weaknesses?

_____

_____

_____

Do you rely on what others think of you? Yes or no? If yes, why?

_____

_____

_____

Are you looking for validation (approval) from others?

_____

_____

_____

_____

Have you ever thought about harming yourself? If so, why?

_____

_____

_____

_____

How are you feeling?

_____
_____
_____
_____

What are you feeling?

_____
_____
_____
_____

What negative or positive thoughts are going through your head?

_____
_____
_____
_____

What areas do you need a push in?

_____
_____
_____
_____

What are your strengths and/or weaknesses?

_____
_____
_____
_____

Do you rely on what others think of you? Yes or no? If yes, why?

_____
_____
_____
_____

Are you looking for validation (approval) from others?

_____

_____

_____

_____

Have you ever thought about harming yourself? If so, why?

_____

_____

_____

_____

Day 10

How are you feeling?

_____
_____
_____
_____

What are you feeling?

_____
_____
_____
_____

What negative or positive thoughts are going through your head?

_____
_____
_____
_____
_____

What areas do you need a push in?

_____

_____

_____

_____

What are your strengths and/or weaknesses?

_____

_____

_____

_____

Do you rely on what others think of you? Yes or no? If yes, why?

_____

_____

_____

_____

Are you looking for validation (approval) from others?

Have you ever thought about harming yourself? If so, why?

How are you feeling?

_____

_____

_____

What are you feeling?

_____

_____

_____

What negative or positive thoughts are going through your head?

_____

_____

_____

_____

What areas do you need a push in?

_____

_____

_____

_____

What are your strengths and/or weaknesses?

_____

_____

_____

_____

Do you rely on what others think of you? Yes or no? If yes, why?

_____

_____

_____

_____

Are you looking for validation (approval) from others?
_____
_____
_____
_____

Have you ever thought about harming yourself? If so, why?
_____
_____
_____
_____

Day 12

How are you feeling?

_____
_____
_____
_____

What are you feeling?

_____
_____
_____
_____

What negative or positive thoughts are going through your head?

_____
_____
_____
_____

What areas do you need a push in?

_____

_____

_____

_____

What are your strengths and/or weaknesses?

_____

_____

_____

_____

Do you rely on what others think of you? Yes or no? If yes, why?

_____

_____

_____

_____

Are you looking for validation (approval) from others?

_____

_____

_____

_____

Have you ever thought about harming yourself? If so, why?

_____

_____

_____

Day 13

How are you feeling?

_____
_____
_____
_____

What are you feeling?

_____
_____
_____
_____

What negative or positive thoughts are going through your head?

_____
_____
_____
_____

What areas do you need a push in?

_____

_____

_____

_____

What are your strengths and/or weaknesses?

_____

_____

_____

_____

Do you rely on what others think of you? Yes or no? If yes, why?

_____

_____

_____

_____

Are you looking for validation (approval) from others?
_____
_____
_____
_____

Have you ever thought about harming yourself? If so, why?
_____
_____
_____
_____

Day 14

How are you feeling?

_____
_____
_____
_____

What are you feeling?

_____
_____
_____
_____

What negative or positive thoughts are going through your head?

_____
_____
_____
_____

What areas do you need a push in?

_____

_____

_____

_____

What are your strengths and/or weaknesses?

_____

_____

_____

_____

Do you rely on what others think of you? Yes or no? If yes, why?

_____

_____

_____

_____

Are you looking for validation (approval) from others?

_____

_____

_____

_____

Have you ever thought about harming yourself? If so, why?

_____

_____

_____

_____

Day 15

How are you feeling?

_____
_____
_____
_____

What are you feeling?

_____
_____
_____
_____

What negative or positive thoughts are going through your head?

_____
_____
_____
_____

What areas do you need a push in?

_____

_____

_____

_____

What are your strengths and/or weaknesses?

_____

_____

_____

_____

Do you rely on what others think of you? Yes or no? If yes, why?

_____

_____

_____

_____

Are you looking for validation (approval) from others?

_____

_____

_____

_____

Have you ever thought about harming yourself? If so, why?

_____

_____

_____

_____

How are you feeling?

_____
_____
_____
_____

What are you feeling?

_____
_____
_____
_____

What negative or positive thoughts are going through your head?

_____
_____
_____
_____

What areas do you need a push in?

_____

_____

_____

_____

What are your strengths and/or weaknesses?

_____

_____

_____

_____

Do you rely on what others think of you? Yes or no? If yes, why?

_____

_____

_____

_____

Are you looking for validation (approval) from others?

_____

_____

_____

_____

Have you ever thought about harming yourself? If so, why?

_____

_____

_____

_____

How are you feeling?

_____
_____
_____
_____

What are you feeling?

_____
_____
_____
_____

What negative or positive thoughts are going through your head?

_____
_____
_____
_____

What areas do you need a push in?

_____

_____

_____

_____

What are your strengths and/or weaknesses?

_____

_____

_____

_____

Do you rely on what others think of you? Yes or no? If yes, why?

_____

_____

_____

_____

Are you looking for validation (approval) from others?

_____

_____

_____

_____

Have you ever thought about harming yourself? If so, why?

_____

_____

_____

_____

Day 18

How are you feeling?

_____

_____

_____

_____

What are you feeling?

_____

_____

_____

_____

What negative or positive thoughts are going through your head?

_____

_____

_____

_____

What areas do you need a push in?

_____

_____

_____

_____

What are your strengths and/or weaknesses?

_____

_____

_____

_____

Do you rely on what others think of you? Yes or no? If yes, why?

_____

_____

_____

_____

Are you looking for validation (approval) from others?
_____
_____
_____
_____

Have you ever thought about harming yourself? If so, why?
_____
_____
_____
_____

Day 19

How are you feeling?

_____

_____

_____

_____

What are you feeling?

_____

_____

_____

_____

What negative or positive thoughts are going through your head?

_____

_____

_____

_____

What areas do you need a push in?

_____

_____

_____

_____

What are your strengths and/or weaknesses?

_____

_____

_____

_____

Do you rely on what others think of you? Yes or no? If yes, why?

_____

_____

_____

_____

Are you looking for validation (approval) from others?

_____

_____

_____

_____

Have you ever thought about harming yourself? If so, why?

_____

_____

_____

_____

Day 20

How are you feeling?

_____
_____
_____
_____

What are you feeling?

_____
_____
_____
_____

What negative or positive thoughts are going through your head?

_____
_____
_____
_____

What areas do you need a push in?

_____

_____

_____

_____

What are your strengths and/or weaknesses?

_____

_____

_____

_____

Do you rely on what others think of you? Yes or no? If yes, why?

_____

_____

_____

_____

Are you looking for validation (approval) from others?

_____

_____

_____

_____

Have you ever thought about harming yourself? If so, why?

_____

_____

_____

_____

How are you feeling?

_____

_____

_____

_____

What are you feeling?

_____

_____

_____

_____

What negative or positive thoughts are going through your head?

_____

_____

_____

_____

What areas do you need a push in?

_____

_____

_____

_____

What are your strengths and/or weaknesses?

_____

_____

_____

_____

Do you rely on what others think of you? Yes or no? If yes, why?

_____

_____

_____

_____

Are you looking for validation (approval) from others?

_____

_____

_____

_____

Have you ever thought about harming yourself? If so, why?

_____

_____

_____

_____

Day 22

How are you feeling?

_____
_____
_____
_____

What are you feeling?

_____
_____
_____
_____

What negative or positive thoughts are going through your head?

_____
_____
_____
_____

What areas do you need a push in?

_____

_____

_____

_____

What are your strengths and/or weaknesses?

_____

_____

_____

_____

Do you rely on what others think of you? Yes or no? If yes, why?

_____

_____

_____

_____

Are you looking for validation (approval) from others?

_____
_____
_____
_____

Have you ever thought about harming yourself? If so, why?

_____
_____
_____
_____

How are you feeling?

_____

_____

_____

_____

What are you feeling?

_____

_____

_____

_____

What negative or positive thoughts are going through your head?

_____

_____

_____

_____

What areas do you need a push in?

_____

_____

_____

_____

What are your strengths and/or weaknesses?

_____

_____

_____

_____

Do you rely on what others think of you? Yes or no? If yes, why?

_____

_____

_____

_____

Are you looking for validation (approval) from others?

_____

_____

_____

_____

Have you ever thought about harming yourself? If so, why?

_____

_____

_____

_____

How are you feeling?

_____
_____
_____
_____

What are you feeling?

_____
_____
_____
_____

What negative or positive thoughts are going through your head?

_____
_____
_____
_____

What areas do you need a push in?

_____

_____

_____

_____

What are your strengths and/or weaknesses?

_____

_____

_____

_____

Do you rely on what others think of you? Yes or no? If yes, why?

_____

_____

_____

_____

Are you looking for validation (approval) from others?

_____
_____
_____
_____

Have you ever thought about harming yourself? If so, why?

_____
_____
_____
_____

Day 25

How are you feeling?

_____
_____
_____
_____

What are you feeling?

_____
_____
_____
_____

What negative or positive thoughts are going through your head?

_____
_____
_____
_____

What areas do you need a push in?

_____

_____

_____

_____

What are your strengths and/or weaknesses?

_____

_____

_____

_____

Do you rely on what others think of you? Yes or no? If yes, why?

_____

_____

_____

_____

Are you looking for validation (approval) from others?

_____
_____
_____
_____

Have you ever thought about harming yourself? If so, why?

_____
_____
_____
_____

How are you feeling?

_____
_____
_____
_____

What are you feeling?

_____
_____
_____
_____

What negative or positive thoughts are going through your head?

_____
_____
_____
_____

What areas do you need a push in?

_____

_____

_____

_____

What are your strengths and/or weaknesses?

_____

_____

_____

_____

Do you rely on what others think of you? Yes or no? If yes, why?

_____

_____

_____

_____

Are you looking for validation (approval) from others?

_____

_____

_____

_____

Have you ever thought about harming yourself? If so, why?

_____

_____

_____

Day 27

How are you feeling?

_____

_____

_____

_____

What are you feeling?

_____

_____

_____

_____

What negative or positive thoughts are going through your head?

_____

_____

_____

_____

What areas do you need a push in?

_____

_____

_____

_____

What are your strengths and/or weaknesses?

_____

_____

_____

_____

Do you rely on what others think of you? Yes or no? If yes, why?

_____

_____

_____

_____

Are you looking for validation (approval) from others?

_____

_____

_____

_____

Have you ever thought about harming yourself? If so, why?

_____

_____

_____

_____

Day 28

How are you feeling?

_____
_____
_____
_____

What are you feeling?

_____
_____
_____
_____

What negative or positive thoughts are going through your head?

_____
_____
_____
_____

What areas do you need a push in?

_____

_____

_____

_____

What are your strengths and/or weaknesses?

_____

_____

_____

_____

Do you rely on what others think of you? Yes or no? If yes, why?

_____

_____

_____

_____

Are you looking for validation (approval) from others?

_____
_____
_____
_____

Have you ever thought about harming yourself? If so, why?

_____
_____
_____
_____

How are you feeling?

_____

_____

_____

_____

What are you feeling?

_____

_____

_____

_____

What negative or positive thoughts are going through your head?

_____

_____

_____

_____

What areas do you need a push in?

_____

_____

_____

_____

What are your strengths and/or weaknesses?

_____

_____

_____

_____

Do you rely on what others think of you? Yes or no? If yes, why?

_____

_____

_____

_____

Are you looking for validation (approval) from others?

_____

_____

_____

_____

Have you ever thought about harming yourself? If so, why?

_____

_____

_____

_____

How are you feeling?

_____
_____
_____
_____

What are you feeling?

_____
_____
_____
_____

What negative or positive thoughts are going through your head?

_____
_____
_____
_____

What areas do you need a push in?

_____

_____

_____

_____

What are your strengths and/or weaknesses?

_____

_____

_____

_____

Do you rely on what others think of you? Yes or no? If yes, why?

_____

_____

_____

_____

Are you looking for validation (approval) from others?

_____

_____

_____

_____

Have you ever thought about harming yourself? If so, why?

_____

_____

_____

_____

Have you had **ENOUGH** of whatever situation you find yourself in? Everyone's situation is different. It can be spouse or boyfriend abuse; or it can be dealing with your parents. It could be molestation, rape, physical abuse, neglect, educational neglect (not sending your kids to school to get their education), emotional neglect, emotional abuse, verbal/mental abuse, domestic abuse, or financial abuse. So, have you had **ENOUGH**?

I don't know what happened to you in your past to make you feel bitter, unloved, mad or hurt, but I humbly want to express my deepest apology for what you may have gone through in your past. Don't let your past ruin your future. Your past can't be altered, so don't punish your future. Take a deep breath, get up and dust yourself off, and start over. Always remember that you are a pearl, and pearls go with everything.

Love,

Ja'Lexis

Connect with Ja'Lexis

:camera: @pearls.thebook

:bird: @PearlsThebook

www.ingramcontent.com/pod-product-compliance
Lightning Source LLC
Chambersburg PA
CBHW071512150426
43191CB00009B/1497